CALCULATOR RIDDLES

Library of Congress Cataloging-in-Publication Data
Adler, David A.
Calculator riddles / David A. Adler ; illustrated by Cynthia Fisher. — 1st ed.
p.   cm.
ISBN 0-8234-1186-9
1. Calculators—Juvenile literature.   2. Riddles—Juvenile literature.   [1. Calculators.
2. Riddles.   3. Mathematical recreations.]   I. Fisher, Cynthia, ill.   II. Title.
QA75.A294   1995   94-41874   CIP   AC
973.73'5—dc20
ISBN 0-8234-1269-5 (pbk.)

CALCULATOR RIDDLES

David A. Adler

illustrated by
Cynthia Fisher

Holiday House/New York

A calculator is a whiz at doing math problems. Most calculators can also be used to write words. That's because eight of the digits when looked at upside down are letters.

Turn on your calculator. (Some calculators use a solar cell and don't need to be turned on.) There should be an O. in the display window. If not, press the C key.

Look at the other keys. All calculators have one key for each digit: 1, 2, 3, 4, 5, 6, 7, 8, 9, and 0. There are also keys marked •, =, +, −, ×, and ÷.

Now take a look at the digits upside down. Many of them look like letters. Press the 8 key. Turn your calculator around. The 8 is now a B. Upside down 3 becomes E. The number 9 becomes G; 4 becomes h; 1 becomes I; 7 becomes L; 0 becomes O; 5 becomes S.

Enter 14 on your calculator. Turn your calculator around. Can you read "Hi"?

Now enter 4509 and then turn your calculator around again. Can you read "GOSH"?

With only eight letters and only eight spaces on most calculators, there are a limited number of words that can be written. But still, you can have lots of fun. You can find the answers to calculator riddles.

First, read the riddles in this book. Then, with your calculator, solve the math problem that follows each riddle. Turn your calculator upside down. The digits will spell a word or words, the answer to the riddle. Of course, since on a calculator there can be no blank spaces, answers of more than one word will run together.

If you have trouble finding the answers to the riddles, turn to page 32.

Have fun!

1. What did Santa say in his garden?

Answer: $190 \times 100 + 19 \times 16 =$

2. Hello! **Hello!**
You still can't hear?
What will make an ear hear?

Answer: $28 \times 8 \div 56 =$

3. If little William ate ice cream, pickles, candy, and sardines, little William would become . . .

Answer:
77 × 100 + 19 × 1,000 − 229 =

4. What's the best answer to someone who calls you a turkey?

Answer: 1000 − 53 × 400 + 9 =

5. What did Jack
say to Jill
after she
tumbled down
the hill?

Answer: 257 × 2 × 50 + 57 × 2 =

6. What was Little Bo Beep's middle name?

Answer: 10 × 10 ÷ 125 =

7. Humpty Dumpty had a great fall. Out flowed the white. Out came the yellow. And what part of Mr. Dumpty could not be repaired?

Answer: 773 × 20 + 9 × 50 + 9 × 100 + 93 =

8. It honks but
isn't a car.
It flies but
isn't a jet.
It floats but
isn't a boat.
What is it?

Answer:

$50 \times 7 \times 100 + 9 =$

9. It's strange. These come in many different sizes but they are always exactly one foot long.

Answer: $53 \times 40 \times 5 + 9 \times 5 =$

10. What do mountain climbers wear on their legs?

Answer: $8 \times 25 \times 35 + 8 \times 25 + 7 \times 2 =$

11. What comes in the middle of every August but in no other month?

Answer: $1323 \div 7 \div 21 =$

12. If 33 is lots
and 66 is
lots more,
what is 21?

Answer: 20 × 55 × 5 + 37 =

13. What happens after
a rude dinner guest
has soup, salad,
hamburger, and pie,
and there's nothing
left to eat?

Answer:
20 × 25 + 31 × 4 × 125 − 33 × 2 =

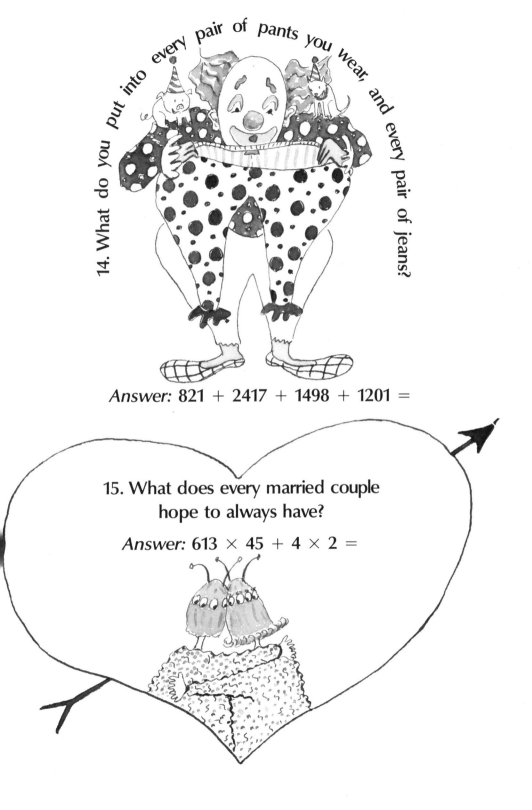

14. What do you put into every pair of pants you wear, and every pair of jeans?

Answer: 821 + 2417 + 1498 + 1201 =

15. What does every married couple hope to always have?

Answer: 613 × 45 + 4 × 2 =

16. George Washington didn't need a bed because he wouldn't . . .

Answer: $35 \times 9 + 2 =$

17. Who invented the telephone but had no one to call?

Answer: $193 \times 20 + 9 \times 2 =$

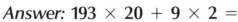

18. What are long, thin, and wet and discovered electricity before Benjamin Franklin?

Answer: $8 \times 80 - 3 \times 9 =$

19. What's the worst thing for a turtle to run out of?

Answer: **200 × 75 + 469 × 50 × 100 + 514 =**

20. What has just three letters but is not small?

Answer: **561 ÷ 11 × 18 =**

21. The fisherman used a lightning rod and hoped to catch an . . .

Answer: $10 \times 10 \times 10 - 267 =$

22. What would you call someone who keeps telling you what to do?

Answer: $20 \times 70 - 23 \times 4 =$

23. What do babies say when they're picked up?

Answer: $9 \times 1001 \div 10 \div 100 \div 100 =$

24. What are made of 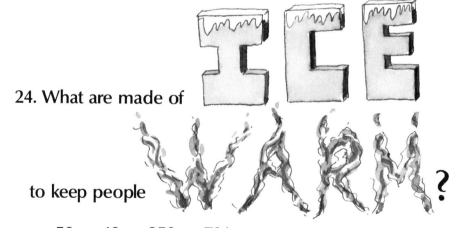 to keep people ?

Answer: $50 \times 40 \times 250 + 791 =$

25. What's the nicest thing you can get a bear who's caught in a trap?

Answer: 50 × 700 + 7 =

26. What can change an ear into a bear?

Answer: **109 × 48 ÷ 6 ÷ 109 =**

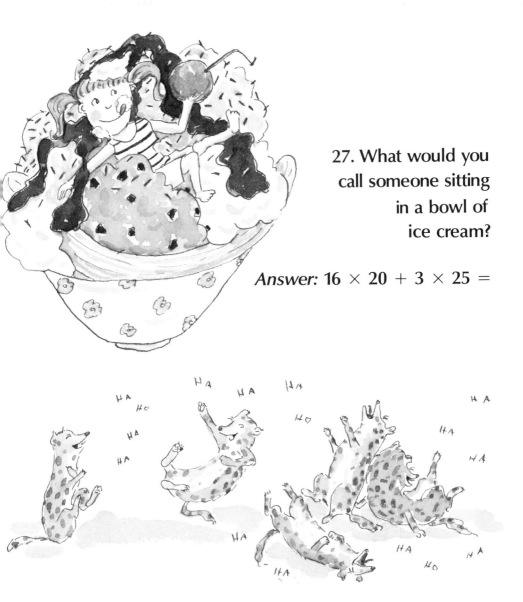

27. What would you call someone sitting in a bowl of ice cream?

Answer: $16 \times 20 + 3 \times 25 =$

28. What do little laughing hyenas do?

Answer: $200 \times 19 \times 100 - 81 =$

29. The runner was fast. He beat hundreds of others in the race. Then he said, "I can't race again. I'm so tired now, I couldn't even beat . . .

Answer: 12 × 50 − 1 × 10 + 3 =

30. What do cute little piglets become?

Answer: $50 - 9 \times 5 \times 16 \times 100 + 51 \times 18 =$

31. What do each of us have two of that a table has more of?

Answer: $25 \times 8 \times 30 - 63 =$

32. You have a big,
heavy bag of beans.
You can hardly lift it.
What can you put in the bag
to make it weigh less?

Answer: $20 \times 125 \div 5 - 37 \times 8 =$

33. A duck opens these a crack and out comes a quack.

Answer: $23 \times 25 + 2 \times 2 \times 25 + 9 \times 2 =$

34. What kind of guns do yellow jackets shoot?

Answer: $100 \times 89 \times 100 - 277 \times 6 =$

35. You don't need a pot. You don't need a flame. This is all you need to make oil boil.

Answer: $129 \times 40 \div 645 =$

36. I have eyes,
a tongue,
and sometimes
a foot.
What am I?

Answer: $25 \times 8 + 3 \times 15 =$

37. Give me a spin. I'm the world we're in. What am I?

Answer:
$47 \times 8 \div 4 \times 5 \times 9 + 1 \times 9 =$

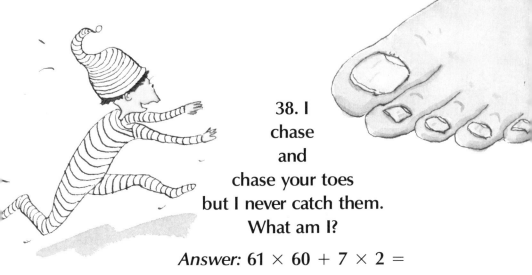

38. I
chase
and
chase your toes
but I never catch them.
What am I?

Answer: **61 × 60 + 7 × 2 =**

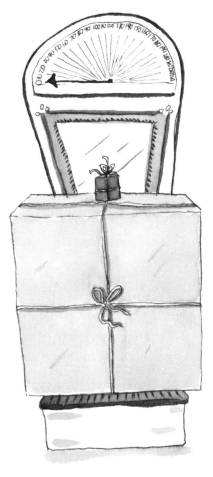

39. I can be big.
I can be small.
But big or small
I weigh nothing
at all.
What am I?

Answer: **20 × 25 − 37 × 8 =**

40. When ghosts chew gum, what
do they blow?

Answer:

$170 \times 20 - 39 \times 200 + 51 \times 8 =$

41. What do little ghosts
get when they fall
down the stairs?

Answer:

$939 \div 3 \times 16 \times 10 \times 100 + 8 =$

42. When friendly ghosts meet they smile,
shake hands and say, "How do you . . .

Answer: $10 \div 125 =$

43. In a restaurant, first comes the hamburger, then the fries and soda. And next comes the . . .

Answer: 100 × 10 ÷ 4 × 16 − 141 × 2 =

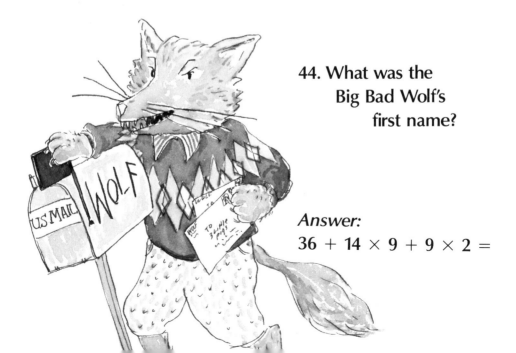

44. What was the Big Bad Wolf's first name?

Answer:
36 + 14 × 9 + 9 × 2 =

45. What's in your bathroom and in your chair
and even after your bath it's still in your hair?

Answer: 98 × 4 ÷ 98 =

ANSWERS

1. 304304, HOEHOE
2. 4, H
3. 7718771, ILLBILL
4. 378809, GOBBLE
5. 51514, HISIS
6. 0.8, BO
7. 77345993, EGGSHELL
8. 35009, GOOSE
9. 53045, SHOES
10. 350414, HIHOSE
11. 9, G
12. 5537, LESS
13. 530934, HEGOES
14. 5937, LEGS
15. 55178, BLISS
16. 317, LIE
17. 7738, BELL
18. 5733, EELS
19. 77345514, HISSHELL
20. 918, BIG
21. 733, EEL
22. 5508, BOSS
23. 0.09009, GOOGOO
24. 500791, IGLOOS
25. 35007, LOOSE
26. 8, B
27. 8075, SLOB
28. 379919, GIGGLE
29. 5993, EGGS
30. 5904918, BIGHOGS
31. 5937, LEGS
32. 3704, HOLE
33. 57718, BILLS
34. 5338338, BEEBEES
35. 8, B
36. 3045, SHOE
37. 38079, GLOBE
38. 7334, HEEL
39. 3704, HOLE
40. 5378008, BOOBLES
41. 5008008, BOOBOOS
42. 0.08, BOO
43. 7718, BILL
44. 918, BIG
45. 4, H